TRUCKING ALONG

The Mack N8 Quantum, produced in collaboration with Renault of France, is the epitome of style, grace and modernity in a cabover truck designed for everyday use in New Zealand at the start of the 21st century. This 'Daily Freight' Mack Quantum with a crisp, yet detailed, colour scheme is operated by JCT Mitchell of Wattle Downs in Manukau City. Seen here far from home in the Manawatu, its driver has his sleeper curtains pulled on a sunny day, perhaps catching a 'kip' after an overnight haul from the north. *Tim Chadwick*

First published 2001, reprinted 2001

GRANTHAM HOUSE PUBLISHING
6/9 Wilkinson Street
Oriental Bay
Wellington
New Zealand

© Tim J. Chadwick
ISBN 1 86934 083 3

This book is copyright, apart from fair dealing for the purposes of private study,
research, criticism, or review, as permitted under the Copyright Act,
no part may be reproduced by any process without the prior permission of the publisher.
Edited by Lorraine Olphert
Typeset and designed by Bookprint Consultants Limited, Wellington.
Printed by Bookprint International Limited, Hong Kong.

One of the new Freightliner Argosy models to hit New Zealand shores in 2000 was 'Touch Too Much', the big green example from Total Transport, operated through Tauhara Haulage of Taupo. The Argosy is seen here at a comfort stop near Pokeno in 2001. *Tim Chadwick*

Opposite page:
Ken Darrah, founder of Reliance Transport in Avondale, Auckland, poses with the company's restored 1953 OLB Bedford. British Bedfords were one of the more popular makes used on New Zealand roads in the 20th century. *Tim Chadwick*
Far right: One of the great US trucking names of the past was Stewart, from Buffalo, New York. Some Stewarts found their way to New Zealand, including this restored 1928 Lycoming-engined model owned by Dave Frandsen of Stratford. *Tim Chadwick*

TRUCKING ALONG

a pictorial history of trucks in New Zealand

Tim Chadwick

Grantham House
New Zealand

Acknowledgments

Stuart Andrews, Taranaki Museum, Pat and Frances Sheen, Alan 'Butch' Banks, Knight & Dickey Ltd, Henry Brown Ltd, Neil Bulmer, Bell Tea Ltd, Brian F. Kilby, NZ Foodstuffs Ltd, J.S. Bolton, Robin and Pamela Chadwick, I. Jim Jones, Joe Bridgman, Tainui Museum, Alexander Turnbull Library, New Zealand Herald, Arataki Honey Ltd, Pam Flack, Wilson & Horton Ltd, Reed Publishing, Archives NZ, Sandy Wullems, Margaret Mort, Hansells NZ, Mark Darrah, History House of Greymouth, J.I. Riddle, Mercury Bay District Museum, Paul Livesy, Fletcher Challenge NZ, Winstones Ltd, Mike Uhlenberg, Sandy Southcombe, Methven Historical Society, Gwen Goodwin, Woodville Pioneer Museum, P.T.L. Transport Ltd, Graham Stewart, Sean Cairns, FBT-New Plymouth, Noel Galloway, Ron Cooke, Taumarunui Museum Trust, Barbara Olsen, Sanitarium Health Food Company NZ, Robyn Donaldson, West Coast Conservancy – Dept. of Conservation NZ, Linda Tancred, John Powell – Kiwi Dairy Company, Gavin Christiansen.

Dedicated to my son Finn

One of the smartest trucks in the huge Owens Global Logistics fleet in New Zealand is this big red Peterbilt cabover, seen here parked at one of Wellington's wharves. The Peterbilt is a long way from home, as it works out of Unsworth carriers' depot in Manukau City, South Auckland. *Tim Chadwick*

So bright it can't be missed is this bright yellow, late 2000 model Scania R144G. The 460-horsepower Scania is one of the many Swedish models imported by Cable Price Ltd. The pictured Scania is owned by Knightrunner Haulers of Wellington. *Tim Chadwick*

The clean, rectangular lines of the big cabover Kenworths seen in New Zealand at the end of the 20th century are exemplified by this mid-yellow one parked in Wellington in early 2001. Compared with the truck drivers of the early 20th century, this driver has all manner of comforts ranging from air-conditioning to a sleeper cab. Modern exterior aspects of this truck are the triple windscreen wipers and mesh window stone guard. *Tim Chadwick*

Two large cabover trucks in repose at Wellington wharves. On the left is a Hall's Refrigerated Transport 2000 model Kenworth, and on the right is an Owens Road Transport Freightliner. Both trucks are awaiting instruction to drive onto the Cook Straight ferry for the South Island leg of their journey. *Tim Chadwick*

Two more 'big rigs' parked up, this time from the US Ford and Freightliner family of trucks, towing tankers. Seen here in the car park of the Furlong Hotel on the northern outskirts of Hawera is a Ford L 9000 from ETL Equipment & Leasing Transport Ltd in Hamilton, on the left, while on the right is a Sterling operated by Shuttle Tankers Bulk Ltd. *Tim Chadwick*

One of the staunchest trucks to 'grunt' its way around New Zealand at the end of the 20th century has to be the big Ford Louisville LTL 9000. This 'King Louis' is a 1992 model, replete with plenty of shiny chrome and operated by Simunovich Fisheries. It is pictured here at the height of summer 2001, keeping the seafood cool, in the Viaduct Basin, Auckland. *Tim Chadwick*

Kenworth trucks are seen all over New Zealand. This is a 1999 T650R model KW, complete with large bullbar, at a comfort stop in the seaside village of Mokau in early 2001. Part of Auckland's Jackson Haulage Company, it is fittingly registered JACK 9. *Tim Chadwick*

A 2000 model Sterling, out of the Freightliner stable of trucks, is seen here in the Taranaki town of Hawera, shifting the old Salvation Army church. The Sterling emanated from Central House Movers Ltd in Bulls, where it joined a fleet of heavy-duty trucks specifically kitted out for moving large buildings. *Robin Chadwick*

Squeezed into the queues of trucks waiting to drive onto a Cook Strait ferry is this newer model Scania 144G. It has come north from its base in Hornby, near Christchurch, where it is part of the Opzeeland fleet. The Opzeeland family has operated this Canterbury trucking business for almost half a century out of Hornby, where it was founded by Cor van Opzeeland and his wife, Helen. *Tim Chadwick*

Renault trucks from France are connected with US make Mack. Renault built trucks throughout the 20th century and has survived into the 21st. One of the latest Renaults for the 21st century on New Zealand roads, incorporating the latest European technology, is this New Zealand Couriers example operated by A.J. and T.L. Howell of New Plymouth. *Tim Chadwick*

Big, gleaming and silver, one of Hall's Refrigerated Transport's New Kenworth K104 Aerodynes for the 21st century, seen here waiting to board the ferry from Wellington in the North Island to Picton in the South Island. It is not uncommon for Hall's trucks to do an Auckland to Christchurch run. The Aerodyne K104 is powered by the Cummins N14 engine of 14 litres capacity, delivering about 525bhp. *Tim Chadwick*

Another truck from the Hall's Refrigerated Transport fleet is this Scania 142M, carrying a load of frozen pork. Scania of Sweden is one of the world's oldest truck manufacturers, having built trucks continuously since 1897. Its first heavy-duty trucks were produced in the 1920s. *Tim Chadwick*

Introduction

RUGBY TRUCKS are Engineered by Experts to Cut Haulage Costs

Rugby trucks in New Zealand were as rare as All Blacks are in the United States. They were built by Durant Motors of Lansing, Michigan, USA, from 1928 until the company was forced to close during the depression in 1932. Rugby engines were supplied by Continental and some of the trucks were built in Canada. A few examples are rumoured to have come to New Zeland, but little evidence remains. *Tim Chadwick collection*

Mechanical transport – the train, the truck, the car, the aeroplane – totally revolutionised the carriage of goods, stock and people from the late 19th century through the global expansion of the 20th century. The origins of the truck can be traced back to French military engineer Nicholas Joseph Cugnot's steam-powered gun tractor of 1769, but it wasn't until the recent 20th century that the truck, as we came to know it, appeared throughout rural and urban New Zealand. Powered by steam, electricity and, more commonly, internal combustion fueled by diesel or petrol, the truck eventually moved through every sphere of New Zealand life, replacing the dray horse as it grew to the size of today's 'big rigs'.

The first trucks arrived in New Zealand a few years before World War I, mainly from England and the United States. They were put to work in cities and towns by companies involved in the transportation of goods to and from shipping wharves and later by breweries, milk-collecting agencies and eventually farmers, who still kept their horse and cart on standby. The First World War sped up the development of the truck in the United States and Europe. The resulting truck surplus after both major world wars augmented New Zealand's national trucking fleet and in the process accelerated the growth of the logging, wool and dairy industries, the building of dams for hydro-electric power and the exploration of oil and gas.

The earliest trucks in New Zealand, such as Leylands from England and Republics and Whites from the USA, were slow-moving machines rolling along on hard rubber tyres. Early drivers had to be one part driver, one part mechanic and one part wheelwright as they faced trucking journeys over not much more than glorified horse tracks or muddy, boggy roads. In the South Island, where alpine rivers could rise rapidly, trucks were sometimes abandoned mid-stream and recovered days later to continue their journey. By the end of the 20th century, seatbelts, air-conditioning, turbo-charging, ergonomically designed seating and a whole raft of changes had totally transformed the truck into a swift and colourful road leviathan hauling huge quantities of product with relative ease. Using pictures and captions, I have attempted to portray the changing shape and character of the truck in New Zealand through the 20th century, including many of the famous trucking names from Mack to Kenworth as well as those that have dropped into the road dust of time such as Commer, Federal, Fargo and Stewart.

Big Caterpillar trucks like the one pictured and other heavy duty makes such as Terex and Euclid are used for off-road dumper work on highway construction in New Zealand. The large tyres and strong hydraulic lifting systems allow these giants of the trucking world to perform in some of the worst terrain nature can throw at them.
Tim Chadwick

In the early days of the 20th century the truck replaced the horse and cart as the prime means for dairy farmers to deliver milk and cream to local factories. Farmers who did not have their own trucks often used the services of truck drivers who collected milk products under contract. Pictured here are the International trucks of early Hawera cream contractor W. Hamilton from the post World War I period. International is one of New Zealand's more enduring trucking names, having seen the whole century through from its origins in the American International Harvester Company and their gas-engined, motorised wagon of 1898. International became an early US market leader after one of its trucks was the first to scale 'Pikes Peak' on 14 June 1916, securing an American military contract in the process. Truly International, the company went on to have its trucks assembled in countries all over the globe.
Taranaki Museum collection

Many of the early trucks on New Zealand roads in the early part of the 20th century were English Leylands. The pictured Leyland, operated by the Opunake Power Board and photographed in June 1923, is typical of the marque at the time with its hard-tyred wheels, New Zealand-built perpendicular wooden cab and gas lanterns for lighting. NZ Leylands of this period were based on the British P-series, developed from the earliest Leyland truck of 1904 commonly known as the Leyland 'Pig' by truckies and engineers of the time! Whereas the 'Pig' had a two-cylinder engine, the P-series was powered by a four-cylinder in-line engine that produced 50bhp. The gearbox was a four-speed sliding mesh arrangement.
Taranaki Museum collection

This solid-tyred P-series Leyland from Wellington, in the post World War I period, was owned and operated by the Wellington Meat Export Company. Built by Wellington builders Munt Cottrell & Co. Ltd, it features a wide-bodied cab and covered rear. Interestingly, the truck has no lighting and virtually bald tyres! The crank handle for starting the engine can clearly be seen beneath the radiator. Pin-striping as an embellishment of the paintwork was popular then, a decorative feature that remained common throughout the 20th century. *Graham Stewart collection*

Two P-series Leyland trucks of the Hawera County Council from around the World War I era. The occasion seems to be a County Council picnic or family outing, perhaps as a Christmas function. *Taranaki Museum collection*

An early 1916 American White automatic dump truck waits on the Mokau wharf in the mid 1920s while being loaded with a cubic yard of roading metal, brought from upriver by barge. On hand is the historic Mokau boat *Cygnet*, which was restored and still running in the year 2000. If only the White were still around too!
Pat Sheen collection

Three P-series Leylands at work on roading near Tongaporutu in North Taranaki in 1922. Beneath the rear truck a worker is placing rocks behind the tyres to help prevent the truck from rolling backwards. Grey papa-clay and dense native bush framed the working day of both truck and driver in this era of North Taranaki roading expansion. *Frances Sheen collection*

Truck driver Harold Hatley leans proudly on the front of his workhorse, a P-series Leyland, in the early 1920s. Leyland trucks were the mainstay of North Taranaki's Clifton County Council where Harold Hatley worked at the time. Note the opening upper front windscreen on the driver's side, the large mudflaps (very useful in papa-clay country!) and the canvas curtain for the side window.
Frances Sheen collection

Newton King Ltd of New Plymouth was one of the early White truck franchise representatives in the early part of the 20th century. The pictured White automatic dump truck, with its stylish convertible hood, gained fame as the first truck to cross over North Taranaki's once infamous Mt Messenger on the main road out of the province to the north. White was one of the most successful early US makes, with its origins in the White Sewing Machine Company of Cleveland, Ohio, in the early 1800s. Company founder Thomas H. White had three sons, Windsor, Walter and Rollin, who pushed for diversity into trucks after Rollin, a Cornell University graduate, invented a steam boiler-powered truck in 1900. The New Zealand photograph of the petrol-engined automatic dump truck (left), by a Mr Barleyman of Waitara, dates from around the First World War. The tyres are hard, solid rubber, and the chain drive is clearly visible.
Taranaki Museum collection

In the South Island of New Zealand, where sheep farming was predominant, the early trucks gradually replaced the horse and cart as a means of getting wool bales from farm to market. Pictured are drivers Charlie Stuart and Billy Weastall with two early American Republic trucks of Stuarts Motors of Coalgate stacked high with wool and about to embark on a slow, steady journey on rugged early Westland roads. The solid-tyre rubber is six inches thick and the lamps kerosene powered. Fully laden on journeys such as these, the Republics were good for 12mph. On occasion, these trucks were known to get bogged down in loose shingle when fording waterways such as South Island's Whisky Creek and the Hutt Stream. A shovel, pick and gumboots were the main components of a Westland truckie's kit in those days. The Republic truck company, in the World War I era, was the largest exclusive manufacturer of trucks in the world, before disappearing in the Depression after the Wall Street 'crash' of 1929. *Reed Publishing*

Photographed in 1918 by early photographer James McAllister, this milk transport truck is thought to be a REO or a Fageol. Note the roll-down canvas sides to the wooden cab area, the wooden spoked wheels and the lack of lights – definitely a daylight operation! James McAllister collection, *Alexander Turnbull Library*

Not all early New Zealand trucks were petrol or diesel powered. Pictured is the Walker 'K'-type battery-electric truck of Percy Bottcher, on his milk run in the Rongotea area of the Manawatu. In 1907 the Walker Vehicle Company of Chicago, Illinois, patented a one-ton battery to power their light trucks which had a four-horsepower electric motor built into the rear axle. Note the large box beneath the chassis where the battery was stored. The wheels are of pressed steel with solid rubber tyres. The most famous of the Walker electric trucks was the one made into a box van for use by Harrods of London in 1919. *Bottcher collection*

A Maori farm worker poses with the early REO farm truck of the Smith family on their Taranaki farm around 1928. The small girl in the picture is Jean Smith, now Jean Andrews, who supplied this photograph. REO stood for Ransom E. Olds, the company founder who had built his first (steam-powered) vehicles in 1886 as Oldsmobiles. They built cars too; the curved dash runabout model introduced in 1901 was America's first low-priced car for the general public. When Ransom Olds sold his interests in Oldsmobile, he formed REO which built mainly trucks. *Andrews Family collection*

Working trucks in New Zealand didn't have it easy as illustrated by this Chevrolet bogged down in deep mud on the Awhitu Peninsula in the 1920s. Driver Ray McNamara appears to be pondering the situation en route to collecting cream for the Waiuku dairy factory, near Auckland. *Knight & Dickey collection*

This Chevrolet 'Superior K' truck from the early 1920s worked for a builder, a Waihi sawmill and later on the farm of the Bridgman family at Athenree in the Bay of Plenty. The Superior-K model was powered by a four-cylinder Chevrolet petrol engine. The truck was restored in the 1990s by Joe Bridgman.

Another early 1920s Chevrolet truck hard at work under duress. This Superior-K model Chevy, loaded with hay on farmland in the Rama Road area of coastal Taranaki, was owned by farmer Alf Bulmer. Unlike the previous two Chevrolets pictured, this one has a split front screen. As with many other trucks, cab configurations for the Chevrolets were agreed upon between the truck buyer and the 'coachbuilder' who usually built the cab from New Zealand timber. *Neil Bulmer collection*

The 'Model-T' Ford, one of the 20th century's universal motoring icons, was also at work in truck form. Allan Bulmer's Model-T, with children Helen, Mary and Neil inside the wooden cab, is pictured in Hawera where he took ownership of the truck as part of the deal when he purchased a carrying business from James Bartlett. Unlike earlier trucks used in the general carrying business, the Model-T of the 1920s had pneumatic tyres.
Neil Bulmer collection

Not all trucks started life as imported chassis and engine cowls with Kiwi-built cabs. Some trucks were made from cut-down cars. This wooden flat-decked farm truck looks to have been made from a cut-down Model-T Ford. The box section on the rear side may be a home-made step to assist people loading the rear, or it may be an early box for a farm dog. *Tim Chadwick collection*

Federal, from Detroit, Michigan, was the producer of some grand American trucks until the company's demise in 1959. The author's maternal grandfather, Thomas Jones, ran a Federal truck from the 1920s in the family monumental masonry business in Hawera. The Jones Bros. Federal put in many hours of hard work carrying gravestones, statues and blocks of rough stone. Federal trucks have quite a strong resemblance to Stewart trucks of Buffalo, a company ironically Federal absorbed before World War II. *Pamela Chadwick collection*

Three milk trucks and their drivers outside the Waiuku Dairy Factory at the start of the 1930s: (from left to right) a Republic, a Chevrolet and a British Bedford, which has a spare tyre strapped to the roof. By the end of the 20th century the old Waiuku factory had become the home base for Knight & Dickey Ltd, a big trucking transport business which took over the premises in the early 1970s. *Knight & Dickey collection*

Havelock North's Arataki Apiaries, the producers of renowned New Zealand Arataki honey, had a 1931 Nash car converted into a flat-deck truck by the company of Ross, Dysart and McLean of Napier. With the truck are Arataki founders Percy and Ian Berry, shifting beehives using what would surely have been Hawkes Bay's classiest medium-sized truck of the era. This early Arataki truck eventually became known as 'Walter Nash', after the NZ prime minister in office 1957-1960. The 1931 model Nash was available with a huge array of engine choice – six different straight-eights of between 3714cc and 5261cc and three different straight-sixes of 3301cc-3983cc. *Arataki Honey collection*

Although it appears to have a large Mercedes-style symbol at the front of it, this truck is an exotic French De Dion Bouton of early 1920s vintage. (The words De Dion Bouton are just visible below the circular grill.) The De Dion, owned by Ogilvie Sawmills, is pictured at Victoria Park, Greymouth, in 1928 where it is displaying an early beach bach or weekend cottage which was being raffled. *Grey District Council Historical Museum*

The early 1930s International flat-deck truck of Hawera carrier Allan Bulmer. At this time the mid-range trucks from the International company had grills and nose sections that wouldn't have gone amiss on many a big luxury saloon car. *Neil Bulmer collection*

Below: The Ford Model-A was yet another of Henry Ford's great models of the first half of the 20th century. Here, the Model-A tow truck of Hawera's H.R. Kemp Motors prepares to tow a rather secondhand-looking earlier Ford Model-T. Note the early AA sign on the tow truck's roof. *Robin Chadwick collection*

A wire-spoke-wheeled Dodge delivery van of the Inglewood Bacon Company from about 1935. Star Brand Bacon, Hams and Lard are advertised on the side, and prospective customers are advised to phone 12 for service! The Dodge is parked outside the butcher's shop in Inglewood with Somerton's tearooms in the background. *Taranaki Museum collection*

A heavy-duty International truck photographed in Hastings in 1932 by the photographer Henry Norford Whitehead (1870-1965). The International belonged to Peter Lowe, a Hastings contractor, who is pictured with the heavy vehicle with its dual rear wheels and strongly constructed steel wheels. *H.N. Whitehead collection, Alexander Turnbull Library (G-4697-1/1)*

The first Bedford truck appeared in April 1931. The British firm, originally from Hendon in North West London, went on to produce some of New Zealand's most popular trucks of the 20th century. Here, an early six-cylinder British Bedford leads the way up a hill near Hunterville in the Rangitikei region, loaded with a stack of baled wool bound for export. *Wilson & Horton collection*

The American Stewart truck company, out of Buffalo, produced some of the classiest trucks of the 1920s and early 30s before being absorbed by Federal. Some came out to New Zealand. Here is an advertisement for the 1934 model. *Stewart Truck Company*

The early side-valve/flathead Ford V8 vans made great company delivery vehicles from their inception, through the World War II era and into the 1950s. Pictured is 'Gertie', the 1935 Ford V8 delivery van of Midhurst butcher Jack Dill. *Jim Jones collection*

More classic photos from the carrier Allan Bulmer. Here, he is pictured with another of Ford's great early trucks, the classic 1938 'Barrell-Nose' model, powered by the side-valve flathead Ford V8 of 3.6 litres. (Bulmer purchased this truck from the NZ army after World War II where it had served as a troop carrier with steel seating boxes on the rear.) *Neil Bulmer collection*

The diminutive 'baby' Austin Seven was also put to work as a delivery vehicle or light truck in the 1920s and 30s. Here, Allan Bulmer poses with his Hawera Milk Supply Austin of only 747cc! Pure Jersey Milk & Cream is advertised on the side. *Neil Bulmer collection*

Replacing the Austin Seven in the early Bulmer fleet was this Standard 9 delivery van of just over 1000cc. Standard of England built popular light vans and trucks from the early 1900s right through to the Standard Vanguard model of the 1950s and 60s. *Neil Bulmer collection*

An example of a Dodge Brothers truck from the 1920s, pictured here at an old vehicle rally at Takaka in 1999. Dodge Brothers Ltd was an American company which became a part of the large Chrysler Corporation. Dodge trucks were built in the US, Belgium and in England. *Robin Chadwick*

Built from a cut-down car, as were many early farm trucks in New Zealand, is this 1928 Pontiac-based, flat-deck farm truck which was owned by Jimmy Ashley of North Taranaki. *Tainui Museum collection*

Photographed around 1940 is this 1937 Chevrolet truck, earning its keep during the haymaking season. Note the opening front windscreen, common on trucks of the period, which helped keep the cab occupants cool (but – also sucked a few bees in!). The '37 Chev truck was powered by a six-cylinder engine. *Andrews Family collection*

This six-wheel-drive World War II truck is a 1943 Studebaker. From 1902-1964 Studebaker built a range of cars and trucks which are now all considered American classics. An old company, founded by the Studebaker family who emigrated to the US from Holland in 1736, its first factory at South Bend, Indiana, in 1852 made wagon wheels. *Tim Chadwick*

When World War II broke out, trucks were put to use by New Zealand and its allies in the war effort. Although a little timeworn, this picture is one of the few left showing a Scammell truck used to haul heavy-duty mobile guns. Scammell of Britain built a range of heavy-duty fairground trucks, snow ploughs and military vehicles in the WWII era, mostly using the six-cylinder 6LW model Gardner diesel engine that produced 102bhp, ideal for towing. The Scammell pictured was part of the New Zealand army's 78th Heavy Battery Unit. *Taranaki Museum collection (L. Beardmore album)*

A large wartime heavy hauler was the American Diamond-T, powered by a big Hercules straight-six petrol engine. Photographed at Wanaka, this Diamond-T model was used mainly for the recovery and transport of damaged tanks during World War II. *Tim Chadwick*

Old and cobwebbed, this angular World War II veteran is a Ford 'Blitz', similar in shape to its Chevrolet contemporaries and built in simple fashion for the war effort. Many of these trucks were assembled by women while the men were at war. Some were assembled in New Zealand, and this Kiwi example, photographed at Wanaka, saw later use after the war as a fire tender. *Tim Chadwick*

Ex-wartime army trucks featured in the books by noted South Island high country author Mona Anderson. From her days at Mt Algidus Station, she recalled this six-wheel-drive GMC truck. Here, it crosses a new section of track by the Wilberforce River, initially washed out by high water. *Reed Publishing*

Here, the same Anderson GMC is seen crossing a shallow section of the Wilberforce. At one stage this truck was caught in rising waters and left submerged for three days before being restarted and driven out. Most ex-army trucks in use in the South Island were imported after the war by G.T. Gillies Ltd of Oamaru, who also imported many spares to keep them running. *Reed Publishing*

This 1942 GMC, now in bright yellow AA recovery colours, is the pride and joy of Shaws Motors in Arrowtown, where, with its long boom and hoist, it is used to pull cars from the Shotover River and from the winding road up to the Coronet ski field. Overzealous winter drivers at the end of the 20th century still had an ex-wartime truck to thank for their recovery! *Tim Chadwick*

Former wartime trucks were also used in the New Zealand logging industry. Here, a large kauri log is hauled out of the Northland forest in the early 1950s by a Helensville company's 'Blitz' which was probably powered by a Ford or Chevrolet engine. *Mercury Bay District Museum collection*

Below: A WWII Chevrolet-powered 'Blitz' which was restored by Ron Anderson, husband of author Mona Anderson, and put to work in the Mt Rolleston and Birdwood Ranges area of the South Island. Pictured with the truck is Ron Anderson on a 'feeding out' mission in the southern snow in the early 1960s. *Reed Publishing*

Below: Ex-military trucks such as the pictured GMC were put to use in South Westland's logging industry after World War II. Here, the brutish GMC willingly fords a South Island river on its way to the mill. *Archives New Zealand collection (AAQA, 6395, 1-M1977)*

Boys from the Whittaker family in North Taranaki pose with the family's rare Diamond-T truck loaded with wool bales. Diamond-T was the builder of some very attractive streamlined trucks as well as blunt heavy haulers. In 1959 Diamond-T combined with Reo to form Diamond-Reo, under ownership of the fellow American White truck company. In turn, the Diamond-Reo make was passed on from White to the Osterlund Company in 1977. *Taranaki Museum collection*

Below: The Wellington-based Foodstuffs Ltd delivery fleet poses with its trucks outside the company warehouse in Martin Square, Wellington, in the late 1940s. From the left is head driver Mac Rouse with his ex-army Ford, Lou Neale with a long-nosed Morris Commercial and Happy Moore with a short-nosed Morris Commercial. These trucks carried goods bound for the early Four Square stores. *Foodstuffs NZ collection*

Another Chevrolet under Pat Sheen's guidance held the record in the 1940s for the most dry sheep skins carried by truck in New Zealand. Here, the truck is parked in New Plymouth with the record 110 skins on its rear deck. *Pat Sheen collection*

Another old Chevrolet. Driver Pat Sheen of the Auckland-New Plymouth daily delivery run poses with his 1937 model Chev in 1939. *Pat Sheen collection*

Whoops! A different driver on the New Plymouth-Auckland run *circa* 1940 ditches one of the Chevrolet 'sixes' en route. Wool bales can be seen stacked beside the road, while some of the other produce lies in a jumble beside a farmer's fence. The only thing injured was the driver's pride. *Pat Sheen collection*

The 1952 season corn bound for the G.J. Watties canneries is harvested into the rear of this 1948 straight-six-powered Chevrolet truck operated by Clare & Clare carriers of Gisborne. *Wilson & Horton collection*

This is a late 1940s relative of the American General Motors Chevrolet firm, the ubiquitous Bedford delivery van from England. The HC model, pictured, was at the time the smallest vehicle in the Bedford range, with a load capacity of just 672lbs. The HC was powered by a 32bhp four-cylinder engine coupled with a basic three-speed transmission. This one was still being used by a Levin panel-beating firm in the 1990s! *Tim Chadwick*

Nowadays owned by Michael Gildea of Dannevirke, this 1947 Chevrolet truck spent most of its life as a very able farm vehicle in the Manawatu. As with other Chevs of the era, the straight-six engine was the most common powerplant. *Tim Chadwick*

A Foodstuffs Ltd Ford 'Jailbar' V8 is here loaded up with 'parcels for Britain', assembled by Foodstuffs in conjunction with the Wellington RSA, to assist with the food shortage in Britain after WWII. The arm of driver Lou Neale is visible in the window, while co-driver Charlie Grant (beside the headboard) and RSA workers tie down the load before it heads to the wharf. *Foodstuffs NZ collection*

An old Ford 'Jailbar' side-valve V8 near the Wanganui River is this example from the late 1940s which was still in active use as a farm truck by John Thurlow, when photographed in the latter part of the 1990s. 'Jailbars', named after their vertical jail-bar-style grills, were produced between 1941 and 1947. Some saw service during World War II. *Tim Chadwick*

Below: This English Fordson is an example of a BP (British Petroleum) tanker of the late 1940s. It is powered by a side-valve-V8 and is pictured at Moturoa, New Plymouth, in October 1949. The names of the workers pictured with the truck are unknown. *Taranaki Museum collection*

The Ford 'Bonus' V8 followed the 'Jailbar' in the medium to heavy-range market sector for Ford from the late 1940s into the '50s. This photo, dating from 1968, shows a Bonus-built Ford at the Okau dairy factory, dropping off cream cans. The truck belonged to Isaac Johnson. *Tainui Museum collection*

Below: The 1947 Fargo owned by Princes Motors, Hawera, proprietor Robert Skedgewell is one of many Fargos imported into New Zealand after World War II. They originated from the Chrysler Corporation factory in Sarnia, Canada (hence the similarities between Fargo and Dodge). The final bodywork assembly was then completed in the Waikato by Hamilton Motor Bodies Ltd. Before being restored by Robert Skedgewell, this particular Fargo worked as a fruiterer's truck in the Stratford area. The Fargo is pictured with Robert, son Gareth and Robert's vintage AJS motorcycle. *Tim Chadwick collection*

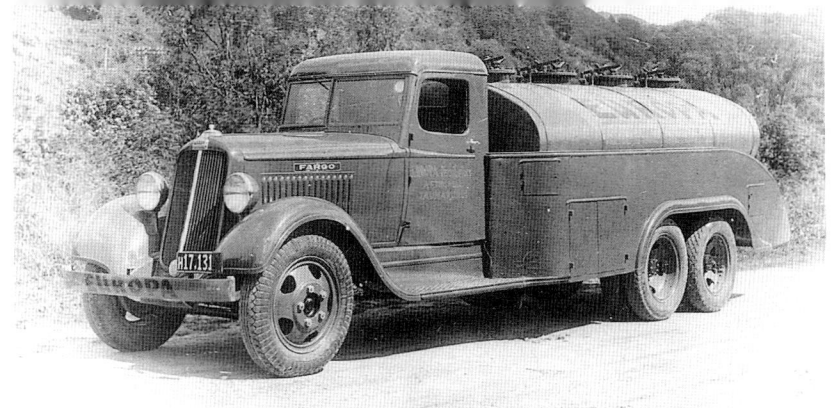

Fargo didn't just build small trucks. Pictured is a much larger Fargo put to work in New Zealand as a Europa petrol tanker. It was the country's first Streamlined tanker and was owned by Taumarunui businessman Bob Tidswell. The Fargo collected petrol in Auckland and delivered it to 22 stations in the Taumarunui-Tokaanu-National Park area. The main drivers were Bill Tidswell, Doug Beever and 'Lofty' Lloyd. *Bob Tidswell*

This page features the wartime and postwar trucks of the Sanitarium Healthfood Company. Below is the late 1930s model Ford V8 truck that worked out of the Hamilton depot. Talented signwriting artists, well before computer detailing came about, hand painted scenes such as the puffed wheat feature on the side of this Ford. *Sanitarium Healthfood Company Ltd*

Below: A front three-quarter view of Sanitarium's 'flathead' Ford V8 delivery truck allows us to see the artist's large Weetbix mural. Note the 'spats' covering the rear wheels. *Sanitarium Healthfood Company Ltd*

In the postwar period Sanitarium operated this smart US-built International KB5, powered by a straight-six engine. The KB5 model was popular when new in the 1946-50 period. Granose biscuits are clearly advertised, with every flake 'A whole wheat grain'. *Sanitarium Healthfood Company Ltd*

One of the smaller Internationals of the postwar period was the K1 model. This example, which was once owned by the grandfather of the author's wife, J. Noel Laird, has been lovingly restored by the Uhlenberg trucking firm of Eltham. Now painted bright red, the K1 'Inter' is powered by its original engine. *Ben Uncles, Mike Uhlenberg collection*

The author's 1950 Jowett-Bradford light truck (model CC). This Bradford was originally a farm truck owned by George Dyer of South Taranaki, with a rear deck built by Spragg & sons Ltd, Hawera. CC model Bradfords, from the suburb of Idle in Bradford, Yorkshire, are powered by a 1005cc two-cylinder horizontally-opposed 'Boxer' engine. They were a direct market competitor with the little English Fordson truck. *Tim Chadwick*

A period photograph of two OLB Bedfords working at the railway line for Winstones Ltd of Auckland. The trucks are being loaded with sand by a Rapier 430 sand shovel. *Fletcher Challenge archives*

The O-series British Bedford trucks became one of the firm's great classics of the 20th century, with the OLB range proving very popular in New Zealand. The Government's Ministry of Works operated many OLBs, including special wellside versions which are now rare. Pictured is the restored OLB wellside truck of Hawera's Moller-Johnson Motors. These days Moller-Johnsons is a busy Isuzu truck franchise holder, but during the 1990s they undertook the restoration of one of the OLBs they sold brand new in 1950! It had originally been operated by a plumber named Bill Phillips. *Tim Chadwick*

Below: The Auckland trucking firm of Reliance Transport Ltd in Avondale was started by Ken Darrah with an OLB Bedford truck. Here, he is pictured in 2000 with a similar 1953 model OLB Bedford restored to commemorate the founding of the company. OLBs were powered by Bedford's reliable 214-cubic-inch, straight-six petrol engine, producing 84bhp. *Tim Chadwick*

A Kew Dodge now residing at a transport museum in Wanaka. These sturdy trucks were powered by a straight-six diesel engine. *Tim Chadwick*

An advertisement for Kew Dodge trucks dating from 1952, so named because they were built at Kew, in Surrey, England. The Kew Dodges were quite popular in New Zealand in their heyday during the 1950s. *Tim Chadwick collection*

One of the many Seddon Mk.5L vehicles now operating in Belgium.

A 3-ton dropside truck. One of a fleet of Seddon vehicles operated by the Iraq Petroleum Co.

At home anywhere!

Not just on the good roads—not just in the moderate climates—not just with the easy loads. Seddon Diesels are at home with any load, in any weather—anywhere! That's their big advantage! Choose a Seddon for your really tough jobs. They never let you down! They save money at every stage during their long life. Our range of trucks for loads from 3 to 10 tons means that there's a Seddon for *your* needs.

SEDDON MOTORS LIMITED

Seddon diesels appeared in New Zealand during the 20th century. Here, we have an advertisement for 3-10 ton carrying models from the early 1950s. In 1970 Seddon took over the Atkinson truck company to form Seddon-Atkinson, which in turn was bought out by the US giant International in 1974. Seddon-Atkinson trucks had a bit of a renaissance on New Zealand roads at the end of the 20th century. *Tim Chadwick collection*

ERF
CONVEYING LOADS OF CONFIDENCE
ALL OVER THE WORLD

The splendid pulling power, stability and economy in running of E.R.F. lorries together with the wide choice of vehicles to suit particular requirements, has inspired a confidence which is being demonstrated by world-wide demands from this dependable range. Agents in most countries—literature willingly forwarded on request.

OVERSEAS AGENTS

THOMAS TAYLOR & GASCOINE LTD., Victoria St., Nairobi, Kenya.
TRUCKS & TRANSPORT EQUIPMENT LTD., Booysens, Johannesburg.
TERRY'S MOTORS (PTY.) LTD., P.O. Box 784, Windhoek, S.W. Africa.
DEPENDABLE MOTORS (PTY.) LTD., 82a-90, Parramatta Road, Camperdown, Sydney, N.S.W.
COMMERCIAL MOTOR VEHICLES LTD., 217, Franklin St., Adelaide.

OVERSEAS AGENTS

BELL BROS. (PTY.) LTD., 117, Swan St., Guildford, Perth, W. Australia.
AIR & MERCANTILE LTD., 20, Brandon St., Wellington, N.Z.
BROWN & CLAPPERTON LTD., P.O. Box 52, Blantyre, Nyasaland.
THATCHER HOBSON & CO. LTD., P.O. Box 92, Broken Hill, N. Rhodesia.
REGENT MOTORS LTD., 32, Cameron St., Salisbury, S. Rhodesia.

The story of ERF is an intriguing one. The company was founded in 1933, after Edwin Richard Foden (ERF) broke away from his family's Foden trucking business in Cheshire, England, after disagreements over Foden company direction. Foden Ltd wanted to stay with steam as the fuel for their trucks, while Edwin saw diesel as the fuel of the future. As history has shown, both companies have survived, in New Zealand as well, on a steady diet of diesel! Above is an ERF advertisement from 1952, mentioning the NZ distributors Air & Mercantile Ltd of Wellington. *Tim Chadwick collection*

An Austin Loadstar, owned by Eric Read, parked on Te Mahoe Road in northern Taranaki. The Austin is carrying a single large rimu log. Loadstars were launched by Austin of England in 1949, and many appeared in New Zealand throughout the 1950s. At the time Loadstars were considered very modern, with their Austin car-frontal styling and three-man seating. They were powered by a straight-six petrol engine that produced 68bhp. *Eric Read, Tainui Museum collection*

The Austin car-like front of the Loadstar can be appreciated in this photograph showing a Loadstar (on the left) at the end of its career, at Horopito, sharing space with another faithful truck of the 1950s, a Ford Thames. The Thames is one of the 4D range which was available in 30 cwt to four tons payload capacity. Engine options included a straight-four diesel that produced 64bhp and an English Ford V8 petrol engine. *Tim Chadwick*

Monarch Motors of Napier operated a V8 Ford Thames tow truck in the 1950s. Here, it can be seen on the Napier-Taupo highway, coming to the aid of a rather stricken vintage Austin that has 'buggered' its steering completely. *Robin Chadwick*

Right: Dating from the early 1950s is this AR110 model International wellside truck. Its longevity is evidenced by the fact that the author photographed it on the slopes of Mt Ruapehu in the late 1990s. *Tim Chadwick*

Left: One of the Australian-built Internationals available in New Zealand in the 1950s was the AS model powered by a straight-six engine. This old but tidy AS was once a light tanker and is now on display at a Wanaka transport museum. *Tim Chadwick*

British Standard Vanguard flat-deck and wellside trucks were popular with business firms and farmers alike through the 1950s and '60s. This one was still being used on a farm near Pipiriki, up the Wanganui River right into the 1990s! Based on the Phase II 'Beetleback' Vanguard, the truck or ute was powered by Vanguard's overhead-valve wetliner four-cylinder engine of 2088cc, which produced 68bhp at 4200rpm. In England the van version was used en masse by the Royal Air Force. *Tim Chadwick*

Below: Spraypainter Bruce Palmer stands proudly beside his 1956 Chevrolet truck, which was still going strong when photographed in 1994. The aggressive forward-looking stance of this Chevrolet was used right through the Chevy trucking range in the late 1950s from the pickup truck (pictured) with the Chevy 'Blue Flame' straight-six right through to the larger heavy-duty range powered by 322-cubic-inch V8s that put out around 215bhp. *Tim Chadwick*

Right: A British Thorneycroft operated by C.P. & P.D. Smith from the Taumaranui area brings a 5,476ft load of rimu out of the 'Waione Skids' in April of 1954. Apparently, the makers of the truck were shocked when they found out that the Thorneycroft was working the logging trails, something it was not designed to do. *Colin Seccombe, Ron Cooke archives*

Above: The first truck of Rongotea's Percy Bottcher, a Walker electric truck, appears earlier in this book and here, we have truck driver Bottcher's last mount, a Bedford truck. This is an A-series Bedford, first introduced in 1953. *Bottcher collection*

Above right: Leyland's Comet was another popular British truck used in New Zealand in the 1950s. Here, a Winstones-operated Comet pulls out of a shed loaded up for its delivery assignment. *Fletcher Challenge archives*

Right: The S-type Bedfords from Luton, England, had a long production life, with minor cosmetic changes along the way, between 1952 and 1969. This is one of Winstone Ltd's heavy-haulage S-type Bedfords, also known as a '12-ton tractor' in its native England. The Bedford is loaded with cement bags. *Fletcher Challenge archives*

Sharing a cab shape with the S-type, the R-type sub-group of this successful Bedford range was the four-wheel-drive variety. The four-wheel-drive Bedfords were used en masse by the New Zealand army right into the 1970s and also found application on 'civvy street'. Pictured here is one of Winstones four-wheel-drive R-types fitted with a hydraulic HIAB masonry hoist. Note the front hubs which give away the truck's four-wheel-drive capabilities and the different grill area from the previous picture of an earlier S-type. *Fletcher Challenge archives*

Below: Some serious wood! By the start of the 1960s this US-built L.174 model International truck operated by Bassetts Ltd of Warkworth held the all-time New Zealand record for carting the largest single log. The kauri log, from Furniss's Bush, Ahuroa, was big enough to create 20,000 feet of usable timber. Are some of those rear tyres looking a little flat on the bottom? *Mercury Bay District Museum collection*

Albion was one of England's older trucking companies when it was taken over by Leyland in 1951. The Albion trucking name continued on until 1972 when it was completely phased out. One of Leyland's Albions was the Albion Reiver LAD-model of 1960. This 10-tonner was powered by a range of Leyland six-cylinder diesel engines that produced between 105 and 125 horsepower, depending on the specification. Here, an Albion Reiver destined for Winstones waits across the road from the Auckland Savings Bank, Economy Meats Ltd and the John Young Dance Studios in Auckland. *Fletcher Challenge archives*

In the 1950s and through the 1960s seven-ton Commer trucks, built by the Rootes Group in England (who had purchased Commer in the late 1920s), were common on New Zealand roads. Here, a '50s 'split-screen' Commer, operated by Clive Cassidy, prepares to ford a stream en route to market, loaded with wool bales from Tautane Station in the Southern Hawkes Bay in January 1964. *Wilson & Horton collection*

The driver of this 1950s seven-ton Commer was lucky to escape with his life when the old wooden bridge he was crossing in rural North Taranaki collapsed beneath the weight of the truck. Many rural bridges in the 1960s and '70s had to be rebuilt or upgraded to cope with the demands of bigger and heavier trucks capable of carrying larger loads. *Tainui Museum collection*

This is a Commer from the early 1960s without the split windscreen of the earlier model. Although sharing the same Commer cab dating from the end of the 1940s in England, apart from the screen, the grill area has been widened to surround the headlights. This Commer from McMurdo Motor Services of Tinwald was put to good use as a tow truck before ending up in Wanaka. *Tim Chadwick*

A photograph of well-known Taranaki truck operator Mike Uhlenberg on the day he purchased the contracting business of New Plymouth's Ken Pardington. The April 1966 photograph also features one of the Commers that came with the business. *Mike Uhlenberg collection*

Waitara's Sonny O'Carroll peers from the side window of his 1958 Karrier. The English Karriers were almost identical to the Commer from the same Rootes Group stable. (Rootes had purchased Karrier in the mid 1930s.) They also shared similar engines, the most common being the 'Sloper-six', a six-cylinder diesel engine lying almost on its side beneath the floor. *Alan 'Butch' Banks*

Winstones also made use of the popular Commer. Here, a company driver prepares to climb into truck number 89, one of Winstones' Commer 'certified' concrete mixers. *Fletcher Challenge archives*

The sturdy British Dodge heavy dumper was produced at the dawn of the 1960s. It was powered by a 5.76-litre, overhead-valve, six-cylinder engine that developed 105bhp at 2,400rpm. The gearbox consisted of five forward speeds and reverse. Pictured is a Dodge heavy dumper operated by Winstones in Auckland in the early 1960s. *Fletcher Challenge archives*

Trucks have played an important role in the aerial top-dressing industry. A Te Kuiti-based Bennett Aviation airtruck is reloaded with fertiliser for aerial top-dressing by one of the Austin-Morris range of its 702-model trucks that usually had a seven-ton load capacity. The Austin-Morris airtruck loading unit is at work here on the farm of Waikawa's Frank Tatham. These 702-model trucks of the 1960s were usually powered by a 5.1-litre, 6-cylinder BMC diesel engine that developed 105bhp at 2,600rpm. *Morrow, Tainui Museum collection*

Operating out of the Palmerston North Foodstuffs depot throughout the 1960s was this Four Square truck, a 1960 Morris five-ton (series-3) truck. It was powered by the 243-cubic-inch, four-litre Austin Morris petrol engine. In 1964 this model was updated, receiving twin headlights and a one-piece windscreen. The horizontal five-piece slat grill was also replaced with a new design. Diesel engines of 5.1 litres were also available for the Morris five-tonner. *Foodstuffs NZ Ltd collection*

An Austin five-ton truck that shares the same body shell with the Morris five-ton once shared duties with a Ford Thames Trader at Arataki Honey Ltd in Havelock North, pictured here in April 1966. The Austin has single headlights and a 'horizontal ladder'-style grill different from the 'Four Square' Morris. The same mechanicals were used, under what has become known as 'badge-engineering'. *Arataki Honey Ltd collection*

The Morris J2 continued the popular line of Morris vans in New Zealand. The J2 started life with the 1489cc, BMC four-cylinder engine and then later received the bigger 1622cc unit. Pictured is the J2 operated by the Bell Tea Company out of Auckland throughout the 1960s. *Bell Tea collection*

Much smaller than the Morris trucks was the quirky-looking Morris J1 delivery van. The J1 was the first in a line of popular Morris vans in New Zealand from the 1950s into the '70s. With sliding doors and outboard headlamps that were outdated for the period, the J1 worked well but at times sluggishly, with its side-valve early Morris Oxford engine of 1476cc, producing 41bhp at 4200rpm. Later examples gained the 1489cc OHV BMC engine. Pictured is an example from Eastbourne, Wellington, still on the road in the late 1990s. *Tim Chadwick*

The Ford Thames Trader was one of the common trucks on New Zealand roads during the 1960s and was available in a range of four and six-cylinder diesel engines or a six-cylinder petrol engine. They usually had a three-ton, 138-inch wheelbase or a seven-ton, 160-inch wheelbase, depending on the application. This is one of Foodstuffs' Four Square 'cargon' delivery Traders advertising "Rawakelle" Tea! The Wingate-based Thames Trader worked well into the 1970s. *Foodstuffs Ltd collection*

Below right: Here, a New Plymouth Ford Thames Trader and trailer unit is used in the top-dressing industry by Taranaki Bulk Topdressers, a forerunner of today's FBT company. The photograph dates from 1964. *FBT collection*

An unusual, smaller-sized Leyland in New Zealand during the 1960s was this 1968 Leyland two-tonner, powered by the 2611cc, straight-six Austin petrol engine. It was still registered and domiciled in the Bay of Plenty in 2000. *Alan 'Butch' Banks*

A Morris truck from the 702 series makes itself useful here in another New Plymouth photograph at the Henry Brown timber yard. Orderman R. Crockett (on the ground) and K.L. Duggan are loading timber. *Henry Brown Ltd collection*

One of the most interesting trucks used in New Zealand in the 1960s was the legendary Foden 'Sandliner'. Winstones Ltd in Auckland operated three of these eight-wheeled trucks from 1961 onwards, carting sand from the Waikato River to the Auckland plant. The steering axles on these Fodens were moved back and other parts of the truck modified to make the most use of axle-load regulations of the era. Powered by screaming 4.1-litre, two-stroke diesel engines that produced 150 horsepower, the Fodens, based on the FE6/24 British model, were a sight to behold (and hear) in the Auckland area. *Fletcher Challenge archives*

A side view of a Winstones Foden 'Sandliner' showing the forward aspect of the fibreglass cab and the front wheels which steered in tandem.
Fletcher Challenge archives

Pacific Trucks originate from Canada. In 1947 the first Pacifics rolled out of a Vancouver shipyard's wharf shed where three British Columbian lumbermen had decided that specialist trucks needed to be built specifically for the logging industry. In 1970 Pacific was purchased by International, but pictured here is one of the classic era Pacifics dating from 1960 which served the New Zealand logging industry around Kaingaroa and Murupara. It is powered by a 400-horsepower Cummins diesel engine coupled with a 15-speed Road Ranger gearbox. This example, now on show at MOTAT in Auckland, is recorded as the first truck in NZ capable of carrying 100-ton loads of timber out of the Kaingaroa forest. *Tim Chadwick*

One of Winstones' smaller helpers from the 1960s is this Tauranga-based JO Bedford three-ton truck. The JO Bedford three-ton was available ex-factory with either a 3,285cc, four-cylinder diesel engine or a 3,519cc, six-cylinder petrol engine. *Fletcher Challenge archives*

'Happily it's Hansells' – and happily for many truck operators it was the faithful and now famous TK Bedford that saw them through the 1960s, '70s, '80s and beyond! Alongside the OLB, the TK Bedford is seen as one of the classic Bedford trucks of the 20th century. Initially launched at the London Commercial Motor Show in 1960, the TK was still being produced in one form or another in 1979. Some countries, such as Australia, with its RLW trucks, produced their own variants. A range of four and six-cylinder engines, producing 64-133bhp, was on offer for the prospective customer with a load range from 3-12 tons, the higher end of the loading being in articulated form. *Hansells NZ Ltd*

TJ-series Bedfords found all sorts of use in New Zealand also. They were popular with the Ministry of Works for roading as well as with many electricity power boards, sometimes in stretched cab format to accommodate several linesmen. The TJ pictured is a four-wheel-drive ground spreader at work for Farmer's Bulk Topdressers in Taranaki. *FBT collection*

'Little John', a TK Bedford owned and operated by Progress Transport Ltd of Piopio, a rural King Country trucking company founded by Bruce Thompson in 1963 and later partnered by Terry Bentham. The ubiquitous TK Bedford was popular in New Zealand in all manner of transport duties including livestock, as pictured. *PTL collection*

Ford's D-series trucks were very common in New Zealand and popular with both farmers and industry. This is one of the D-series Fords owned by Arataki Honey Ltd of Hawkes Bay. *Arataki Honey collection*

Well into the 1960s Leyland Hippos were still at work in New Zealand. The Hippo was originally the six-wheeled standard version of the 'twin-steer' Leyland Steer, and a rigid eight-wheeler was marketed fittingly as the Leyland Octopus. These Leylands were powered by a straight-six Leyland engine developing around 125bhp through a five-speed transmission. This example is driven by John Burgess, bringing rimu out of the Puketapu 3-A block near Taumarunui for the Waipari Timber Co. on a road known as 'The Punga'. The general manager of Waipari, Laurie McDowell, follows along in his Mk III Ford Zephyr. *Colin Seccombe, Ron Cooke archives*

This is a 1965 International RDF 195, owned and operated by Sandy Southcombe at Bell Block in North Taranaki. The Taranaki Building Removers' rugged International was still operating at the start of the 21st century. Powered by an 8V53 Detroit diesel, the truck is named 'Philp's Pride' in honour of the International RDF's previous owner, J.R.Philp. *Sandy Southcombe collection*

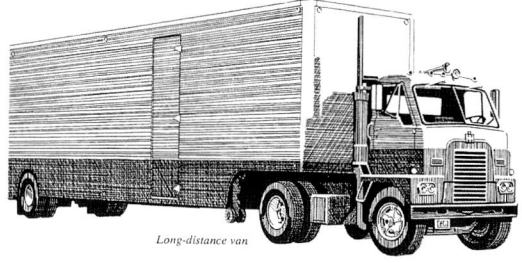

An advertisement for International trucks in the 1960s shows two of the popular models of both 'cabover' and nosed trucks on offer from this successful US-based company. *Tim Chadwick collection*

Pictured in 1970 is this White dump truck operated by Mike Uhlenberg, working out of Eltham. This particular White was brought into New Zealand by Cable-Price Ltd and worked on the Kaimai tunnel project in the Bay of Plenty, when operated by Kevin Mawlor. It was powered by a V6 Detroit diesel engine, producing 210bhp. *Mike Uhlenberg*

Similar to the International in the advertisement is this International Fleetstar 2010A, photographed in 1976 and owned by Te Puke trucking legend Stan Williamson. Originally V8 petrol powered, it was converted to a six-cylinder CAT diesel engine. *Mike Uhlenberg*

Another US-built Fleetstar 2010A model International is this example operated by Mike Uhlenberg, haulage contractor, out of Eltham. Although the A designation means this truck was also originally petrol powered, it was later converted to a 250bhp Cummins diesel. *Mike Uhlenberg collection*

By the 1970s the first wave of Japanese trucks was starting to break the British and American monopoly on New Zealand trucking. Pictured here in front of Mt Egmont/Taranaki is a split-screen cabover 1970 Nissan diesel tanker towing two 2000-gallon milk tanks for the Moa Cooperative Dairy Company in Inglewood. *Moa collection, Kiwi Dairies Ltd*

Early large-sized Mitsubishi trucks were marketed worldwide as Fusos. This is a Fuso T810 stock truck of the mid-1970s, operated by Woodville Freighters Ltd, taking part in a town parade in 1975. T810s were available with Mitsubishi diesel engines of 132-265bhp. *Woodville Pioneer Society collection*

German Mercedes-Benz trucks have played an important part in New Zealand trucking history, finding all sorts of constructive use here. Pictured is one of their larger models dating from 1970, these days employed as a mobile house-truck at gypsy-style fairs. *Tim Chadwick*

Here, a smaller Mercedes-Benz (model 1113) is used in the rural top-dressing industry by Mike Uhlenberg Haulage of Eltham during that company's dabble in pasture-spreading through the 1980s and '90s. Mercedes-Benz trucks of the period were typified by their rounded snouts! *Ben Uncles, Mike Uhlenberg collection*

A state-of-the-art, square-cabbed Mercedes-Benz ground-spread truck from the start of the 21st century is typified by this (model 1834), 'Merc' photographed in 2000. It is owned by B.F. Hughes Transport of Manaia. *Tim Chadwick*

Logging trucks throughout the latter part of the 20th century often carried their empty trailers 'piggy back', as typified by this big White 4000 from Napier, photographed in the early 1980s. The White 4000 was the forerunner of the popular White 'Roadboss'. *Mike Uhlenberg*

Volvo of Sweden has been building trucks since 1928. It was also the first European company to offer turbo-diesels, back in the early 1950s, and the first to offer American-style cabover designs back in 1962. The pictured cabover design dates from the dawn of the 1980s and was operated by Ohakune Transport. *Mike Uhlenberg*

No truck book would be complete without a few Kenworths! Although known originally for their conventional 'nosed' trucks, they also built some popular cabover models. This cabover model dates from the 1970s but was still seeing service in the 1980s with R.J. Olsen Ltd of Lower Hutt. It was originally owned in New Zealand by Uhlenbergs Ltd of Eltham. *Mike Uhlenberg ollection*

This is a cabover Mack operated by Refrigerated Freightlines Ltd in the 1980s. The RFL fleet was always recognisable in its blue-and-white livery. *Mike Uhlenberg*

Photographed in June 1981 is this TM Bedford from Senior Transport Ltd in Auckland. The TM model was launched in 1974 but was still seeing world service well into the '90s. Detroit Diesel and Cummins were the usual engine suppliers for the TM Bedfords. *Mike Uhlenberg*

Dented from hard work with Hawera roading contractor Fred Kumeroa, this English Dodge from the early 1980s is seen here at work on one of the author's car sheds in the early 1990s. The Dodge is based on the Commer Commando range that appeared in 1974, shortly before the Commer name disappeared altogether in 1976. Some versions were also marketed in the UK as Karriers. *Tim Chadwick*

A rare trucking name in New Zealand is Oshkosh who have specialised in logging trucks, snow ploughs, and heavy-haulage vehicles in their native USA. This is a powerful 8V-92T Detroit Diesel-powered Oshkosh that was operated by Mogal Rigging in the 1980s during construction of the synthetic fuel plant at Motonui, south of Urenui. *Sandy Southcombe collection*

One of the most common Macks seen in New Zealand at the tail end of the 20th century was the R600 series, with its friendly but purposeful appearance. Far from home is this Manukau Transport Mack R600, photographed in Miramar, Wellington. *Tim Chadwick*

'The Big Mack' of the 1980s and '90s was the staunch square-grilled Superliner. Pictured is a Superliner parading the NZ Americas Cup yacht KZ7 through one of Dunedin's main streets in August 1986. The spire of Knox Church is in the background. *Tim Chadwick*

An NZL Transport Mack Superliner tows a 128-wheeled, 16-axled trailer loaded with a 31-metre-long, 173-tonne urea reactor, headed for the Kapuni amonia urea plant from New Plymouth. This photo was taken at Midhurst by the author's father, a urea plant worker, in 1996. *Robin Chadwick*

At the rear of the same 128-wheeled trailer load was the rear-steer vehicle, a Scammell (complete with ballast tank) belonging to Inglewood Motors. Scammell is a British heavy haulage specialist usually offering engines from Cummins or Rolls Royce. Leyland engines were also once offered by this long-standing company, founded back in 1922, which produced the world's first 100-tonner in 1929. *Robin Chadwick*

Many of the Internationals on New Zealand roads in the latter part of the century were of Australian origin. Pictured is one of the Australian designs, a T2670, operated by Reliance Transport of Avondale in Auckland. Over the years, since the inception of the T-series in the late 1970s, the cab has remained cube-like but the grill and bumper area have gradually been updated. In Australia some Atkinsons are based on the T-series.
Tim Chadwick

Above right: Another popular Australian-sourced International has been the S-series, typified by this Farmers Bulk Transport International S2600 operated by Bell Block's Shane Christiansen. It rolled off International's Melbourne assembly line in 1987 and has to date covered over 1.6 million miles on New Zealand roads, powered by a 400bhp Cummins diesel engine. *June Christiansen*

Small or mid-sized cabover Kenworths appeared in New Zealand throughout the 1990s. These were the L700 series, powered by Cummins C11 engines of around 300bhp. Pictured is an L700 working as a dump truck on the outskirts of Tauranga in 2000. *Tim Chadwick*

Mid-sized cabover Macks were also brought into New Zealand in the 1980-90s. These were predominantly the European turbo-charged 'midliner' G260 Macks built by Renault and designed in the late 1970s. *Tim Chadwick*

Right: Cummins 400 powered is this unmistakable Kenworth, sporting the classic conventional Kenworth nose section. Operated by NEALSAM of Mt Maunganui, this truck represents one of New Zealand's best-loved truck shapes of the second half of the 20th century to come out of America. *Tim Chadwick*

At the turn of the century Swedish Volvo trucks were still out in force on New Zealand roads. Here a flatbed FH12 model operated by Te Kauwhata Transport tows a similar flatbed trailer. *Tim Chadwick*

As the trucking industry grew in New Zealand towards the end of the 20th century, truckstops or diners that offered space for truck drivers to park their rigs appeared on all main highways. Pictured are a Freightliner and an ERF ('Heaven On ERF') from Taranaki, parked at a diner on the outskirts of Te Kuiti in the King Country. *Tim Chadwick*

Below: Operated by L.R. Hughes of Army Bay, Whangaparoa, for the huge Owens Transport group, is this big Freightliner tanker. Freightliners originated from Salt Lake City in Utah, USA, with the Consolidated Freightways Company in 1939. The first trucks hit production straight after WWII in a Portland, Oregon, factory. Freightliner was once involved with both White and Volvo but at the turn of the century is owned wholly by Mercedes of Germany. *Tim Chadwick*

Peterbilt was founded by timber businessman T.A. Peterman after he purchased the remnants of Fageol in 1939. Eventually, Peterbilt became a sister company of Kenworth and went under the umbrella of the Paccar group before the century ended. Uncommon in New Zealand, the classy Peterbilts are keenly sought out by 'truck-spotters'. As the number plate in the picture shows, this Uhlenberg Haulage Peterbilt is powered by a 550 CAT engine. This particular Peterbilt was built in Texas in the late 1990s and imported by Uhlenbergs from Vancouver, Canada. *Ben Uncles, Mike Uhlenberg collection*

Delivering an underground fuel tank for a new Caltex service station at Bayfair, Tauranga, in 2000 is this 1997 model Freightliner FL112 owned by NZL Transport. These models were usually powered by a Cummins M11 400bhp diesel engine. *Tim Chadwick*

ERF trucks were still going strong at the end of the 20th century. This pristine dumper, rigged out for heavy loads, is an ERF EC11 owned by Cascade Mining of Westport. It has a 400-horsepower engine allied to a 15-speed gearbox. In New Zealand ERF, MAN (of Germany) and Western Star (USA) are under the same franchise holding. *Sean Cairns collection*

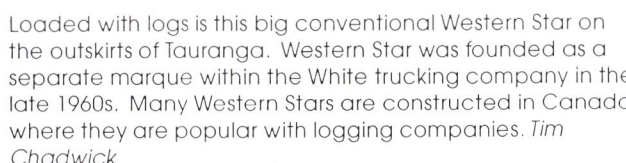

Loaded with logs is this big conventional Western Star on the outskirts of Tauranga. Western Star was founded as a separate marque within the White trucking company in the late 1960s. Many Western Stars are constructed in Canada where they are popular with logging companies. *Tim Chadwick*

Right: Nissan Diesel started out in 1935 as Nihon Diesel of Japan, using two-stroke diesel engines. Today they are a major Asian trucking firm, servicing all sectors of the trucking industry in New Zealand. Here, a Central Cranes Ltd Nissan Diesel passes by the Copthorne Hotel en route to a waterfront building site on Auckland's Jervois Quay during the Americas Cup building boom at the turn of the century. *Tim Chadwick*

Above: Seddon-Atkinson trucks with their distinctive, circled big A symbols were still on the roads in New Zealand at the end of the 20th century. Here, an Emmersons Ltd, Seddon-Atkinson Strato model plies its trade near Alton in South Taranaki, far from its home base in the Hawkes Bay.
Tim Chadwick

You can't keep an old Kenworth down! – especially when it still has plenty of work to do. What's more, this 'Kenny' is fitted out as a heavy-recovery tow truck, on 24-hour call in Palmerston North. Heavy-recovery trucks usually find themselves bringing home other equally large trucks that have broken down or been damaged in the line of duty. This Kenworth is operated by McGinty's Towing Service. *Tim Chadwick*

Below: An oldie but a goodie – the sturdy historic Pacific P9 of McCurdy Engineering is a grand example of one of these 'no-nonsense' Canadian trucks, still performing its duties at the end of the 20th century. McCurdy Engineering is based on Devon Road in New Plymouth and, like Inglewood Motor's fleet of trucks, is known for its preservation of the Pacific marque. *Tim Chadwick*

Close to 20 years old, the powerful aspect of a White 'Roadboss' rarely goes unnoticed! This sparkling example of one of the US White company's finest, works on Cat-diesel power and is seen here towing a load of logs through the Bulls intersection, in the Rangitikei. This great example of a White is operated by B.K. Maby of Feilding. *Tim Chadwick*

This is a late 1990s Freightliner cabover in NZL Transport colours, bringing shipping containers into the Port of Auckland at dusk, near Mechanics Bay. The Freightliner is operated by Aldridges of Cambridge. *Tim Chadwick*

Below: Part of the updating of the truck range produced by International (The International Harvester Company) in the late stages of the 20th century saw the introduction of the new American-style Navistar Eagle range of trucks to New Zealand. Here, an Eagle hauls petroleum product for Mobil Oil Ltd through Manukau City in South Auckland in December 2000. *Tim Chadwick*

Ian Roebuck Crane Hire of New Plymouth runs a fleet of vehicles out of its Auckland depot situated in the harbour area not far from the Americas Cup berths in the Viaduct Basin. One of its useful trucks is this Foden, from the long-standing British trucking firm founded in Sandbach in 1887. The photo was taken in January 2001. *Tim Chadwick*

Milburn Cement is one of the country's large cement companies that couldn't exist without strong reliable trucks. In Wellington Milburn is served by several trucks, including these conventional Volvos from Sweden. These two are Volvo N10 models, the front vehicle dating from 1988 but still earning its keep in 2001. *Tim Chadwick*

Big Macks have always found plenty to do in the heavy-haulage line. This is one of the Superliner-styled conventional cabbed Macks working under the 'Multi-Trans' banner and is operated by M.J. Templeton of Papakura. It is pictured at Westgate's New Plymouth wharf where it shifted massive pieces of machinery from Fitzroy engineering onto a huge barge bound for the Maui offshore oil platform in January 2001. *Tim Chadwick*

The mid-range trucks are just as valuable in serving New Zealand industry and society as the 'big rigs'. Many of the roles required in the mid-range trucking niche are filled in New Zealand by Japanese trucks. This Isuzu FUR-12H is no exception, a product of the Japanese company that started way back in 1916, manufacturing vehicles under license from Wolseley of England. The pictured Isuzu works in our capital city as part of the Wellington Works Infrastructure team. *Tim Chadwick*

The long-serving TK Bedford is probably the greatest all-round truck used in New Zealand in the 20th century. Although the model was launched in 1960, it was produced until the end of 1984, and many examples of the faithful British TK are still seen on our roads in the early part of the 21st century. Quite a few still work in the top-dressing industry around the country, as exemplified by this very tidy TK working for Hamilton's 'SuperAir' out of the Te Kuiti airfield. *Tim Chadwick*

The pride of the Mitsubishi truck range in 2000-2001 has been the big Shogun model. They have been popular with big city firms such as Reliance Transport in Auckland and with operators in rural areas, showing their versatility. Here, 'piggy-backing' its logging trailer in the lower North Island, is the bright-liveried Mitsubishi Shogun of Burling Transport of Masterton. *Tim Chadwick*